NOT JUST ANOTHER COMPUTER BOOK

Revision 1

by

Prof. Alfonso J. Kinglow

PREFACE

After reviewing many computer books over the years, I discovered that they all assume that the reader's have some basic knowledge of computers and that they understand the entire computer lingo's that are used. All of their assumptions are wrong, and lead sometimes to misconceptions. This new Revision takes into account the new Windows OS Windows 10 and all of the new Software and Utilities now available to users that were not available during the first publication in 2014. Since then Technologies have changed and new Technologies are now available to the users to allow them to monitor and troubleshoot their own hardware and software. New hidden utilities and hidden Codes in Windows 10 are presented to empower users to explore and investigate. New and Free Software and Utilities are available on the Internet, where to go and get them is presented in this Revision.

Almost all of the computer books I reviewed did not have, or did not include basic computer terms used, or did not explain the meaning of some basic computer concepts.

This book assumes nothing, and tries to present basic computer information in a plain and simple format, which includes some hidden features and commands that all users should know; but are not published. These hidden features are basic information built into the hardware and software that are in the public domain; but are not considered important enough for the readers to know.

This book gives the user a complete knowledge of computer hardware and software and current related standard's up to date with this Revision.

An emphasis is placed on current and new standards that applies to new technology today, and why they are important. I review the current Wireless Standard (**802.11 b/g/n**) and the new Standards **ac,** and **ad.**

We also explain the "defacto" standards that are used in today's technologies.

This basic knowledge help's the reader to understand why some hardware and software features that are used operate the way they do, and explains the difference between standards related to computer networks, hardware and software.

The material presented provides an in-depth of introductory computer subjects; which includes how to use computers, how to access information and data on computer networks and the Internet World Wide Web, and hidden features and commands embedded into your computer hardware and software and basic information on Microsoft new Windows 10 operating System.

The objectives of this Revised book are to:

1. Present the most up to date Computer Technology
2. Teach the basic concepts of hardware and software
3. Present the material in a way that Seniors and Users can understand it, using basic simple comprehensive methods, Charts and Graphics.
4. Present a basic understanding of Local Area Networks (LAN) and Wide Area Networks (WAN) and Wireless Networks.
5. Present basic information on how to secure your computer
6. Present the most up to date Technology on computer security hardware and software in **Windows 8** and the new **Windows 10** with the new changes in the operating system.

7. Give students and users an in-depth understanding of why computers are used in business, academia, government, industry and society today.
8. Present strategies that seniors and users can use to install secure and maintain their desktop and laptop computers.
9. Present some of the hidden software and utilities in Windows 8 and in Windows 10.
10. Show the users how to use SNAPIN's and the Microsoft Management Console (MMC).
11. Present information on Free and Paid Antivirus Programs
12. Present information on how to use Email and Email Applications.
13. Present complete and comprehensive information on the Internet and the World Wide Web.
14. Present information on setting up Wireless Networks and using WI-FI on the Internet with the new Standards 802.11 AC and AD.
15. Complete information on using the Internet Search Engines and Search operators.
16. Present information on Free Software available for Download
17. Present information on Freeware, Shareware, Trialware and Public Domain Software.

DEDICATION

I Dedicate this book to all of the
Seniors at Munson Senior Center in
Las Cruces; New Mexico and Shadow
Mountain Senior Center and Paradise Valley
Senior Center, in Phoenix, Arizona

Who showed interest in learning about
Computers and
Attending my Basic and Intermediate
Computer Classes

And for the
Cooperation of all the Staff at all the Centers
for their help and attention in assisting me and
providing all the necessary space and facilities
for the classes at the Centers, and to
Genevieve, Guillermina, and Sally, in Las
Cruces, who encouraged me and supported
my vision to make Technology available to
Seniors, and many others, for their support
Thank you

ACKNOWLEDGEMENT

To my wife Sarah Elisabeth
for all her support, love and care
and for

My Strength
My Light and
My Joy
My Daughters
Kezia, Keren and Karina

Who inspired me to leave some of my vast
knowledge behind for posterity
and

For my Grand-son Kenny, "Te-Sho" Virtue
and Longevity
and my
Grand-daughter "Aia" Anaiah, Patience,
Purity and Power

This first Book is for you. You all made me a
very proud Father, Grandfather and a better
person, now and forevermore.

Limit of Liability/Disclaimer of Warranty

===

Disclaimer

CHAPTER 1
UNO

Any computer consist of three major parts, the input, the output and the ALU. The input is the keyboard, the mouse, a flash drive, the Ethernet or Internet connection, a microphone, a camera, etc.. Anything that enters data into the computer using one of the many computer ports. The output is the video display, or video monitor, the printer, a video recorder, etc.. The ALU is the arithmetic logic unit which contains the CPU, central processing unit, the memory, or random access memory called RAM, the storage hard drive or HD and the OS or operating system.

The operating system or OS is part of the Software, and the rest of the components are part of the Hardware. Your computer operation will require using both the hardware and the software together.

They are minimum Hardware requirements in order to efficiently use the Software OS. The minimum requirements also will affect the User Software programs that will be installed on the computer.

Most computers will already have the Software OS such as Windows 7 or 8 already installed with some User Software. Most of the User Software will be Trialware, there will be some free Games and Utilities installed.

Trialware software will only have limited capabilities and will only work for a period of 30 to 60 days sometimes, some Trialware software do not install the complete version of the software and only a basic portion is installed, after the trial time; the user will be required to purchase a license to install the full version of the software. The Trialware version will then have to be un-installed correctly in order to remove it safely from your computer before you can install the full license version of the software.

It is recommended that you install a full version of the software you want to use and not install Trialware software on your computer. Your computer may also come with a Trialware version of some kind of Antivirus software.

It is very important to note that the Trialware version of the Antivirus program will not fully protect your computer. After a short period of time you will also be required to purchase a full version of the Antivirus program.

You may install in the mean time a Free version of any Antivirus program; such as (.AVG) which is a Freeware Application. This will provide some Basic protection to your system, until you can install a complete Antivirus program.

The Free AVG Antivirus is a complete antivirus application, with the basic necessary modules to protect your computer. You may purchase the full application at any time which will give you more capabilities and protection. It is better to install Freeware Applications than any Trialware Application. You may also find many Public Domain Software that are very useful and are also free.

If you are looking for applications and utilities for your computer, you may find useful software in Public Domain, Open Source, and Freeware Software on the Internet. All these categories contain software that are free to use and download, and are not " Trialware".

CHAPTER 2
DOS

Minimum Hardware Requirements for your Computers.___

Your computer hardware must have the following minimum requirements in order to run more efficiently software applications and the (OS) Operating System, such as Windows 7 or 8.

1. Processor INTEL or AMD 2.0 Ghz to 2.8 Ghz or higher
2. Ram-Memory 2, 4, 8, or 16 Gigabytes, ODD memory is unacceptable such as 3Gb or 6Gb or 12 Gb. Ram Memory must always be EVEN   (1-2-4-8-16-32-64Gb) etc..
3. Hard Drive Storage should be 500Gb to 1 Tb (Terabyte) internal, however; you may also have an External USB drive of 1 Tb or higher for Backup or to extend the storage capacity of your computer.

The recommended Software OS should be the Basic standard version or the Professional version of the software. Windows 8 Professional is far better than Windows 8 Home, Student or Basic editions. Windows 8 operates in 32 bit mode or 64 bit mode. Sixty four (64 Bit) mode is faster and is recommended if you are going to use more than 4 Gb of Ram Memory. Windows 8 in 32 bit mode works just fine if you have 4 Gb of Ram Memory or higher.

New users to Windows 8 will notice that the OS does not have a START button. If you would like to have a Start button, because you are familiar with this capability from previous versions, you may install one.

- The Windows 8 Start button is a free application that is available on the Internet, other free applications are also available for download at several web sites. You may do a

Search on Freeware Software and Public Domain Software to get these applications and or utilities.

Almost all of the free applications and or utilities provided on a CD that is available from the Author of this book will work with Windows 7 and or Windows 8. It is recommended that you upgrade your computer to Windows 8. The new Windows 8.1 Upgrade removed the Start button and other basic components from the Desktop. It is recommended that you stay with Windows 8 until the new Windows 9 is released. Since very soon Windows 9 will be coming out, it will require some review. The Windows Operating System is evolving very quickly to provide the users with better and faster technologies.

Please note that we the users are the one's that are driving the technology, we are demanding better and faster hardware and software. We want more and faster applications and multimedia software. Large Software companies such as Microsoft Corporation, and other's; are trying to keep up with the user's demands.
We are now using more social media applications to communicate via the internet, such as Facebook and Twitter, and these companies are also trying to keep up with the user's demands.

Computers are now a necessity and are required in every household in America and elsewhere, as a very essential tool for business and or entertainment.

The speed of your computer will depend on the type of processor in your computer, with the amount of Ram Memory installed.
INTEL is the largest manufacturer of Computer Chips and Computer processors in the World, followed by AMD and others.

Intel Dual-Core Processors i-5, to i-7 are very fast processors and are now available in some laptops and desktops computers. It is recommended that you get a computer with one of these processors, with a storage capacity of at least 500 Gb minimum, up to 1 Tb. Internal hard drive.

Below is the basic layout of a Computer showing the ALU Arithmetic Logic Unit that contains the Memory, Storage and Operating System with the CPU Central Processing System, the heart of the Computer.

It is recommended that the Computer have an Intel Processor with a minimum speed of 2.5 Ghz (Gigahertz) and 8 Gigabyte of Ram Memory to run Windows correctly with all its modules.

CHAPTER 3
TRES

The Bit and your Computer Processor Speed.__

The smallest unit of information that can be transmitted over the internet or to and from your computer is called a Bit.

The Bit is a binary number that represents 0 (zero) or 1 (one).

Using just these two numerical characters you can transmit any message you want to a computer since every letter in the alphabet
has a binary equivalent sets of numbers, representing 8 bits.; such as 01100111. Since bits are very small they had to be divided and organized to handle large amounts of **Data** to facilitate **Storage** and distribution.

So, 8 Bits is equal to *1 Byte* and 8 Bytes is equal to *1 Word* .

The following terms are therefore used in all Computers to designate thousands and millions of Bytes: *Kilo-bytes* is equal to one thousand bytes, *Mega-Bytes* is equal to 1 Million bytes, *Giga-bytes* is equal to 1 Trillion Bytes, *Tera-bytes* is equal to 1 Billion Bytes, etc.. These values are used in computers for storage and to designate computer memory.

In the case of designating Processor speeds, a different term is used to represent cycles per second or (cps) which is also designated in hertz, used in the name of the German Physicist that discovered it. So we say that processor speeds are measured in cycles per second or (cps) or we can also say in hertz or (hz).

The speed of processors are always in Giga-hertz or Giga-cycles per second (Ghz). A fast processor should be above 2.0 Ghz per second. Anything below 2.0Ghz will be very slow. A processor speed above 2.0Ghz will be very fast. Fast computers have processors that are 2.5 Ghz to 3.0Ghz or higher., To achieve very fast speeds, processors are built with Dual-Core, which will have more that one processors. Some computer manufacturers chips will contain dual core processors running seven (7) or more processors and are designated with the "I" Code, such as Intel Processor Dual-Core i-7. To get a fast computer, make sure you meet the above requirements of a fast Processor and a very large storage for your data. Most computers will have at least a storage hard drive of at least 500 Gb (Giga-bytes) of storage or higher. You can now buy external hard drives for storage in the tera-byte range. In designating computer memory, a division was selected to facilitate operation and distribution of in line memory modules that were single or dual so thay could be used in various types of computers. These memory modules were called (SIMM's) or single in-line memory modules, and (DIMM's) Dual in-line memory modules, and Random access memory or (RAM). Memory used in computers were divided as 1, 2,

4, 8, 16, 32, 64 Gb (Giga bytes) of Ram memory or higher, always EVEN MULTIPLE numbers to meet computer standards. Computers with ODD MULTIPLE numbers are not acceptable, because the computer memory is shared with other parts of the computer such as the Video Display, not leaving enough memory for the system and or applications, and may not fully meet US or International Standards. Such computers are sold with 3 Gb of RAM memory or 6Gb of RAM memory; and are unacceptable.

Computer Hardware. ___

Computers in general are divided into two parts, Hardware and Software. Hardware contains all the major parts of the computer such as the hard drives, The CD/DVD drives, the processors, memory and all the computer input ports such as Printer port, USB port, video port, and keyboard and mouse.

The computer hardware depends on the installed memory, storage drive and processor speed necessary to work with the Windows OS Operating System.

With the hardware and the Windows OS also is important to note the Accessories. Some of these Accessories are built-into the Hardware and Software. Some of the most important Hardware utilities that are built-in are:

Hardware Security utility; Hardware Management, part of the hardware management is the Command Line CMD.

The hardware System Utilities that includes The Firewall and

Defrag, and the User Utilities that contains the Notepad,

WordPad and others.

The Hardware Security Utility contains the MMC and the hardware Snap-Ins., one of the most important utility built in to allow the user to manage and setup the Security and Configuration of the Computer.

The most important ports on your computer are; the USB ports, most computers will have 2 or more USB ports. USB is a standard that replaces the old computer ports that required large and cumbersome connectors and were very slow sending data back and forth to your computer. USB 2.0 became a defacto standard and was implemented several years ago into every computer hardware. It is very fast sending and receiving data. A USB cable which is thin with the flat USB connector is required to connect almost any device you wish to connect to your computer and it includes cameras, keyboards, Web cams, mouse, etc..

A new USB standard was released last year, its USB 3.0 which is faster than USB2.0 and almost all new computers now have this standard implemented into the hardware. It requires a USB 3.0 cable which is downward compatible to USB2.0

Software.__

Software are the Programs that make all of the Hardware work. The major software in any computer system will be the OS or Operating System such as Windows. The other major software will be the Applications and Utilities. Some software will need to be installed by the user and some will be installed by the OS or Operating System. Major user software will be the Applications such as Microsoft Office, and others that will facilitate the users to become more productive. Utilities will protect the computer from threats and viruses.

Software programs in general are divided into the following areas: Software Applications, Productivity, Games, Development, Multimedia, Educational, Utilities, System, LAN Local Area Networks, Web Software, Maintenance, Network, Paint, Accessories, Programming, Basic, Communications, Cloud Software, WAN Wide Area Network (The Internet), Graphics, Antivirus, etc...

Software programs are Installed, Deleted, Removed, and Purged.

When a Software program is Installed, it must be Un-Installed.

When a software program is Deleted, it must be Un-Deleted.

To correctly remove Software Programs, it must be done in the Control Panel in Programs and Features, if you are running Windows 8. The program is then Uninstalled or Changed. Dragging a program to the Trash or Recycle Bin does not Remove it, to Remove a program it must be Shredded in the Recycle Bin.

To Destroy a program it must be Purged.

Most Software are in the following modes, Virtual Software, Hyper-V Software, Free Software, Search Software, Shared Software, Open Source Software, Public Domain Software, License Software, Encrypted Software, Decrypted Software, Cipher Software, Network Card Test Software or (loop back address Software), OS Windows Software(Operating Systems); Firewall Software, Security Software(Bit Locker), Printer Software, Email Software, DSL Router Software, etc..

Software Languages and Standards. __

Most Software are written in the following computer languages: Hypertext, used in Web Browsers on the Internet, Unix, Basic, Ada, C and C++ (C Plus Plus), Html (Hypertext Markup Language), Xml   (Extensible Markup Language), Fortran, Pascal, and High Level Compilers, etc....

The Standards that govern Software are: Defacto Standards, IEEE Project 802.x, The OSI Model and the ISO (International Standards Organization).

The Seven Pillars to Execute Software Programs.__

1. Setup and Install the Software
2. Uninstall and Undelete
3. Add and Remove
4. User Install and System Install
5. Run, Search and Delete
6. Free, Trial and Test
7. Open Source and Public Domain software access

Search Software Formats. __

The following Search Software Formats are used on the Internet as follows:

Search with --------→ AND or + -------→ Red Cars and Red

Vans.

Green Apples +

Red

Apples.

Search with -------→ OR ----------→ One word to be in search

(Flight

Attendant OR

Stewardess.)

Search with ------→ AND NOT (-) -→ suv AND NOT auto

(suv –

auto)

Search with ----→ Phrase Searching --→ Exact Phrase within

" Harry Potter"

Quotation.

Search with ----→ Wildcard ---→ WRIT* CLOU*
-→ The

Asterisk at
the end of words.

SEMANTIC SEARCH ENGINES ON THE INTERNET.

1. **DuckDuckGo**

2. **Dogpile**

3. **WebCrawler**

4. **Ask.com**

5. **Hakia.com**

6. **Momma.com**

What is a Semantic Search Engine.___

Semantic Search and the Semantic Web

While *Semantic Web* and *Semantic Search* are not the same thing, the two concepts are often confused.

The fact that these two families of technologies share the word *semantic* has led to some confusion about the difference between them. According to Merriam-Webster, semantic means "of or related to meaning." Both of these kinds of technologies attempt to retrieve and present information based on its meaning rather than on its structure or intended usage, as more traditional technologies do. Although they are related, the two technologies in fact solve different problems.

In brief, **Semantic Search** is useful for searching on a single type of data in a single domain, whereas **Semantic Web** technologies are useful for querying <u>across many types of related information</u>. Consider a few examples of each kind of technology.

Although Google generally does a good job in ranking web pages, most of us know that this kind of search completely fails in other contexts. For example, searching your own computer for a document by relying on keywords can be very frustrating—not to mention searching a data store the size of your corporate intranet! In such cases, you will not succeed unless you know exactly what you are looking for. This shortfall is not the fault of the technology itself;

This is where Semantic Search comes in. Rather than blindly returning anything that contains the text you typed into the search bar, Semantic Search takes into account **the *context* of your search** as well as **the underlying meaning of the documents to be searched.**

However, what if you were searching for *jaguar*, the predatory black feline? Or JAGUAR, the Mac 10.2 operating system? Or JAGUAR, the Atari system? Even on Google, straightforward keyword searching <u>does not take into account the context of your search, nor does it understand the meaning of the documents.</u>

In an attempt to do a better job, Semantic Search technologies employ various methods (NLP, statistical modeling, etc.), to categorize and/or cluster related documents to ease searching.

Semantic Web.____

The Semantic Web is a set of technologies for representing, storing, and querying information. Although these technologies *can* be used to store textual data—such as text in a Word document or PDF file—they typically are used to store smaller bits of data. Thus, while Semantic Search focuses largely on textual information, **the Semantic Web** <u>also includes numbers, dates, figures, and other data in addition to text.</u>

Semantic Web and Semantic Search Combined

Generally speaking, anything that can be accomplished with Semantic Search can be represented as a Semantic Web query. That is, Semantic Web technologies are sufficiently broad to encompass all Semantic Search capabilities.

A simple way to think about which family of technologies might be useful for a specific problem is to ask yourself whether your users are searching on only one kind of information (e.g., restaurants, a flight number, etc.), or whether they are searching on many kinds of information (e.g., which presidents had children who did not live in the White House).

Semantic Web vendors focus on solving problems using many different kinds of information. Instead of simply storing data about restaurants, a Semantic Web application would have access to information about the chefs, the cities, the menus, the cuisine styles, the décor, the wine list, the wineries that produced the wine on the wine list, etc.

However, if you need to answer a question such as, "**What restaurants in Boston have several wines that were produced in the Alsace region between 1998 and 2001?**" then Semantic Search will not be able to help you; instead, <u>you will need the</u> **<u>Semantic Web</u>**.

Hardware.__

The Hardware is the box or frame that contains all the major parts of a computer, the internal hard drive, the CD/DVD Player, the different input ports, the keyboard and mouse, the processor and ram memory, the Ethernet network card, the Wireless network card, the video display, the LCD display(on laptops), the sound card, the internal built in camera, the internal microphone, etc.. One of the major Ports is the USB (Universal Serial Bus) that is now used to connect Printers, Cameras and multiple other devices to your computer hardware.

Policies are built into the computer hardware to allow for security and to manage the hardware. Some of the most important policies are the SECPOL. MSC (Security Policy) and GPEDIT. MSC (Group Policy Editor) these policies allow you to setup the security configuration on your computer hardware. These policies are launched using the Command Line (CMD) built into your computer, or by typing the policy directly into the START or RUN line. The Command Line CMD is provided as a means of accessing your Computer Hardware and Software policies and to directly manage a great part of your computer hardware, without requiring any software to manage policies.

It is used also for direct maintenance of the computer and comes with a reasonable help file. This file contains all of the commands used with the CMD. The command line window when launched appears with a black background. The background and text colors can be changed from a menu of different colors as well as the text size and window size. Some preferred combinations are; red background with yellow text color or green background with white or purple text color, etc... To change the color background and text, click on the cmd icon in the upper left side of the command window.

To access all of the standard policies to set up your computer hardware you can find them in the MMC (Microsoft Management Console) built into your computer hardware.

The MMC allow the user to create SNAP-IN's to setup the hardware and security configuration. To access the MMC just type it into the CMD window or directly into the START or RUN line, on the lower left side of your computer.

A View of Computer Configuration with Applications and Utilities. ____

The User Tools and System Tools are presented in a Graphic configuration easy to understand. All the Diagnostic Tools that are built-into Windows are shown and are available to the user, for diagnostics and troubleshooting the computer.

Twelve Diagnostic Tools are shown that are built into Windows. All these tools can be access by the user. If the Computer is running Windows 10, just type in the name of the tool in Cortana, to access, or just type the name into the Start area for all other Systems.

CHAPTER 4
CUATRO

Your Computer hardware Ports and your Desktop. ___

Most computers will have the following standard hardware ports; a printer port, the CD/DVD port, the mouse and keyboard ports, the microphone and audio ports, at least three to four USB ports, the video port, the Ethernet port, the power input port. The USB ports will serve as external ports to connect multiple devices, such as an external Hard Drive or external camera or Webcam.

Your computer hardware ports have *designated hardware symbols* to identify each port. A list of these hardware symbols are contained in this book. Each symbol is imprinted on the external hardware case to identify the port. These symbols meet international standards for hardware identification ports and some have become " *defacto standards.*"

Your Desktop. ____

Your Desktop is one of the most important parts of your computer. When you turn on your computer it will boot up and display your desktop window. Your desktop will have a background color or image that can be changed by the user. Your desktop can get corrupted and it is very important to keep your desktop clean from clutter. Having many icons on your desktop will create clutter and take up storage space.

Protected Folders on your Computer._____

Special folders were created to keep your user documents and personal files, in order to keep them organized and off your desktop.
Such folders that are protected are: The *Documents folder*, the *Music folder*, the *Pictures folder*, and the *Videos folder*.
Some icons are required to be on your desktop so that they can be accessible immediately by the user and the system, such as: *My Computer*, *My Network* and *Internet Explorer* or IE.
If you need to put a copy of documents, pictures or other files you use daily, then you should put them into folders, if they are going to reside on your desktop; and not leave the icon open on your desktop. You could also create " *shortcuts* " of your documents and or applications or any other files you wish to leave on your desktop, instead of leaving the original document or image.
Shortcuts do not take up a lot of space or memory. Your desktop icons can be changed in the Control Panel in " *Personalization.*"

Laptop computers vs. Desktop computers vs. Notebook computers. ___

Laptop computers were designed to be mobile, containing a battery that would provide from two to four hours of continuing use, and provide all the software and connections necessary to allow the user to work in a wireless environment. Laptops are now fabricated with great processor speeds and large amounts of memory and storage. Desktop computers are the more traditional form of computers built to be fixed in a home or office environment containing very large boxes with many drives and devices. These hardware boxes are generally heavy and are called " *chassis*" and they contain very large power supplies and storage drives that are heavy.

Notebook computers are usually very light and just have a basic operating system designed to provide the most minimum capabilities and connections. They are also limited in processor speed, memory and storage capability. Some notebook computers are now been built with similar capabilities like laptops, with very fast processors. The most popular laptops and notebooks are made by HP (Hewlett Packard), Toshiba, Samsung, and others.

The Task Manager.__

Since computers are Task driven machines, and operate by tasks and processes, a Task Manager was built into the OS to manage and organize computer tasks for the user. Sometimes the user will overload the computer with multiple tasks at the same time, and the computer will freeze or crash as it runs out of memory trying to perform all of the tasks requested by the user. Sometimes the users will assume that computers are multitasking machines and they forget that to do multi-tasking, any computer must meet the following minimum criteria:

- Must have large amounts of memory (8, 16, or 32 GB)
- A very fast processor (Intel dual-core I-5 to I-7 or higher)
- A large storage area (500 GB to 1.5 TB) Hard Drive

The Task Manager will also allow killing a process that hangs causing the computer to freeze, and also allowing the user that is logged on, to " disconnect himself" from the computer without login off.

You can access the Task Manager two ways: From the keyboard, press down at the same time, CTRL+ALT+DEL keys,

And also with the CTRL+SHIFT+ESC Keys. The Task Manager will also show applications that are running, all of the Background processes as well as all of the Windows processes.

It will also show all of the applications that have an impact when your computer startup, and the services that are running in Windows.

The Antivirus Software Program on your Computer._

All computers must have at least a basic Antivirus software program installed on the computer to provide protection against Viruses. Beware of Security programs that are available and claim to protect your computer from viruses, to protect your computer from viruses, you will need to have a full paid version or a basic Free version installed and configured on your computer. The Antivirus Software program should Scan your computer after it has been installed, your computer must be connected to the internet only to get the Virus Definition File Update. The Virus Definition File updates your Antivirus program software, so that any known viruses or late published threats, will be known by your Antivirus program, before you run a Scan. Normally after the installation is done your Antivirus program will automatically connect via the internet and update its Definition file before running a Scan.

Once your Antivirus is updated, the next time you run a Scan on your computer; you must be disconnected from the Internet. to disconnect you may turn off your Router or Disable your Ethernet and or Wireless Network Adapters in the Control Panel. Once the scan is completed and no viruses are found, you can re-connect your computer to the Internet or turn back on your Router and or Network Adapter cards.

Run your Antivirus program at least once a week. And keep your Virus Definition File up to date.
Many Antivirus programs exist; the most popular paid versions are made by: Norton, MacAfee, Panda and others.
The Free basic Antivirus that is very popular is made by AVG.
AVG Antivirus can be downloaded from the Internet for free as well as others.

Both the Free versions and the paid versions will provide the protection you need. Do not connect your computer to the Internet if you do not have an Antivirus program installed on your machine. Beware of Trialware Antivirus programs that come with your computer, since they will expire in 30 to 60 days and do not offer any protection to your computer, since they are not a full version of the original software and do not contain all of the software modules. Most of them have no Virus Definition files to update.

When Antivirus Programs do not work.

Most Antivirus programs will not work if their Virus Definition File (VDF) is not up to date.

A View of Computer Viruses in Graphic Format. ___

Below is a graphics presentation of all the Viruses and what they do. The worse being the Rootkit and Hoax Virus.

A new Virus type have emerged called : "RamsonWare" a type of virus that takes over the computer and ask for a Ransom, then the user must pay a large amount of money, to get the computer released. The FREE programs work fine.

Any program that is written to harm your Computer is considered a Virus.

Only an Antivirus program or Application can get rid of Viruses in Computers.

Programs that are labeled " Computer Security" does nothing to eradicate Viruses. An Application called an " Antivirus" is the only program to eradicate Viruses.

Popular Antivirus programs are AVG, Panda Antivirus, etc,, Some are FREE and some are not.

COMPUTER VIRUSSES.—

VIRUS — PROGRAM THAT SPREADS BY REPLICATING ITSELF INTO OTHER PROGRAMS.

WORM — SELF REPLICATING, BUT DOES NOT ATTACH ITSELF. A SELF CONTAINED PROGRAM.

TROJAN — PROGRAM APPEARS TO BE USEFUL BUT CONTAINS MALWARE, EJ. A UTILITY.

MALWARE — ANY SOFTWARE PROG. DESIGNED TO CAUSE HARM.

HOAX VIRUS — WORSE KIND OF VIRUS, SENDS HOAX MESSAGES TO USERS.

ROOT KITS — FORM OF TROJAN, MONITORS TRAFFIC TO AND FROM YOUR COMPUTER, AND ALTERS SYSTEM FILES.

SPYWARE — AFFECTS EMAIL, MONITORS AND CONTROL PART OF YOUR COMPUTER, DECREASE COMPUTER PERFORMANCE

SPAM — A NUISANCE, NOT A THREAT, ITS UNSOLICIT MAIL (E-MAIL) (ED)

ADAWARE — LIKE SPYWARE, AFFECTS COMPUTER PERFORMANCE

CHAPTER FIVE
CINCO

LIST OF VIRUSES.__

Here is a list of the most common viruses, and what they are:

- VIRUS a program that spreads by replicating itself into other programs or documents.
- WORM a self-replicating program, like a Virus, but does not attach itself. It's a self-contained program.
- TROJAN a program that appears to be useful, but its not; and contains MALWARE , for example: A Utility
- MALWARE Any software program designed to cause harm to your computer.
- HOAX VIRUS The worse kind of Virus, it sends hoax messages to users, from the infected computer.
- ROOT KITS a very dangerous form of TROJAN, it monitors traffic to and from the infected computer, altering the system files and infecting other computers on the network, without the users knowing.

- SPYWARE affects email, and monitors and control part of your computer, by decreasing the computer performance considerable, and infecting your email contacts.
- SPAM a nuisance, not a program and not a threat, its unsolicited mail via email.

Protecting your Computer from Viruses. _____

You can protect your computer by installing a free or paid version of an Antivirus program. Many Antivirus programs are available from different manufacturers, they all protect your computer when properly installed, and with the Virus Definition file updated. A first time Scan is required before the program can begin to protect your computer. Before you start the next Scan, after you have done your first Scan, make sure that you are disconnected from the Internet, and or turn off momentarily your router. Then you may Scan your computer again.
The first time you Scan your computer you need to be connected to the Internet so that your Virus Definition file can get updated.

It is advisable to Scan your computer at least once a week.

A Security software program is not an Antivirus program and does not offer any protection against the many viruses that are a threat. Some Security software programs claim to protect your computer from viruses, only an Antivirus software program will protect your computer from viruses.

Your Computer Security. ___

Windows 7 and 8 comes with some security protection. The new Windows 10 operating system have a new complete security configuration that is presented here as part of the Revision.

They are two main Security modules in the Control Panel, one of them is called; Windows Defender and the other is Windows Firewall. Make sure that they are both turned on and are working. Your Firewall must be always on to protect your computer from threats.

Firewalls can be internal or external, and can be software and or hardware. Having an external Firewall box will greatly enhance the security protection to your computer.

The Control Panel in Windows 7 - 8 and 10. __

The Control Panel is the heart of your computer. All the modules running in the Control Panel are performing a function so that your computer may run smoothly.
To access the Control Panel, go to the Start or Run button in the lower left side of your Desktop, and select Settings, if the Control Panel is not visible in the menu, to bring up the Control Panel or if you are running Windows 8 you may also go to the Folder on the lower left side of your Desktop, and click on Computer, and the Control Panel will be displayed in the center Tabs that are visible. The Control Panel Icon Folder is unique and very different from any other folders.

Administrative Users vs. Standard Users

In the Control Panel one of the most important controls is the User's Control Panel, where you can Create new Users for your computer and edit existing users. It is recommended that you first create a New User, when you get your computer for the first time. This New User would most likely be you. Once the user is created, you need to give the New User Administrative Rights, so that the user may have full control of the Computer. This user will then become the User Administrator. A Standard User will not have rights and privileges on the computer to do anything. As the Owner of your computer, you need to have full rights on your machine. Otherwise you will not be able to install or remove any software or do basic maintenance on your own machine, so this is a very first most important step, after getting your computer.

System Administrator vs. User Administrator

It is very important to know what is the System Administrator Password. If the Windows System Software gets corrupted, and needs to be re-installed; you will need to know the Administrator Password in order to get into the System to perform general maintenance and reinstallation of the system software. When Windows is installed for the first time on any machine, in the installation process, a password is requested for the *Administrator*, this password is important to know and remember, if you did not install your system and some one else did it; then you might be out of luck if you do not know the Administrator Password or Admin password. Most computers come with the Windows OS already installed, so the Admin password is not known. It is therefore important to get the original Windows Re-installation DVD, so that you may reinstall Windows if it gets corrupted or crashes.

Every new Computer should be provided with the Installation DVD included in the "sealed" Box and not in a Box with a Tape over it, which indicates that the Box was opened, and that the original DVD, Manuals and other User Documentation was taken out. Please note this as it is obvious that the Computer was not shipped to the store in a box with a Tape around it. All Computers are shipped in "sealed" boxes, there is no Tape involved.

The User Administrator only has rights and privileges over the user's machine and does not have any System administrator rights over any of the System software.
If the user tries to change, alter, modify etc.. Any system applications; a message will be displayed alerting the "User" that he or she does not have any rights or privilege to make or do the changes they want.
Please note that the User with Administrative privileges is not the same as the User Administrator.

CHAPTER SIX
SEIS

COMPUTER NETWORKS, NETWORKING AND THE COMPUTER NETWORK CARDS OR ADAPTERS.

Let us define what Computer Networks are first, any computer that is connected to any other computer to share files and other applications is said to be connected to a Network. When computers need to share files and other software they are connected together in a LAN. A LAN is a Local Area Network. To facilitate this configuration, all computers have built in Network Cards.

They are two kinds of Network Cards also called NIC's, The first card or NIC is the " Ethernet Card" This is a special card that meets the International Standard for Networking called Ethernet (IEE 802.3) or Project 802, which is an IEEE Standard, accepted worldwide. The speed of this network card is 100 Mbps or 1 Gbps.,(Gigabit Ethernet) or higher.

The Gigabit Ethernet card is much faster than the 100 Mbps card and is desirable.

WIRELESS CARD OR ADAPTER. __

The second Network card is the Wireless card or WiFi card **(802.11b/g/n)** and the new standard **ac/** and **/ad.**
So the built in Wireless card should be (802.11 b/g/n or 802.11 b/g/n/ac or ad. This is the new Wireless Standard for the Network card that is preferred if you want to have a fast Network connection. If your Wireless card does not meet this standard, then it will be very slow and you will not be able to connect to the Internet. Your Wireless built in card must be at least (802.11 b/g/n) or higher.
Computers connect to the Internet through these cards. The connection to and from these cards is called Networking.
The settings for your Wireless and Ethernet cards are in the Control Panel, and it's called: "Networking and Sharing Center".

Networking is divided into LAN (Local Area Networks) and WAN (Wide Area Networks); The largest WAN in the world is the Internet.

Wireless adapters or cards are also installed into Printers which makes them " Wireless Printers" Most printers are now Wireless and require no cables, most printers are supplied with a USB (Universal Serial Bus) Cable, which is another Standard used in computers and networking.

WAN Networking requires special equipment and meets different standards with different kinds of cables and interfaces.

THE NETWORKING MODEL

Networking is based on a Model accepted worldwide; it's called the OSI Networking Model or Open Systems Interconnect. Computer Network cards and Networking in general must follow this Model. All network cards are assigned a network protocol number or network ID that identifies the card on the Network. It is a special hexadecimal number (numbers and letters combined), this is also called in networking an IP (Internet Protocol) Address. This IP identifies the computer on a Network and is part of the Internet Protocol (TCP/IP) a Networking Standard. Without a TCP/IP address number the computer can not connect to the Internet or Network.

The speed of the computer Internet connection will depend on the built in Network cards. To find out what kind of Network cards is installed in your computer; go to the Control Panel to Network and Sharing Center and select "change adapter settings" to display the type and kind of network cards installed in the computer.

Networks and the Internet. _____

Networks are used to join computers and devices together and to share resources. The type of resources that are shared are: Information, Hardware, Software, and Data.

A Hardware resource that is shared could be a single connected Printer, that is shared via the Network to multiple Computers. These are shared through a LAN (Local Area Network) or a WAN (Wide Area Network.)

To access the Internet services the user can connect via an ISP (Internet Service Provider) or via an OSP (Online Service Provider).

The main Internet Service is the World Wide Web (www.) and the Internet is the largest Network in the World.
The Internet is a worldwide collection of Networks that links individuals with resources and Data. The Internet have Millions of users and is growing more and more every day. The Web contains Billions of Documents called Web Pages.

The Internet Web Page Link. ___

A Web Page on the Internet may link to other Web Documents, and to Text, Graphics, Sound and Video.
A Web site (Google) may contain a collection of related Web Pages. Computers store Web Pages and the user, can use a Web Browser such as IE (Internet Explorer) or Firefox to view them.

The content of those Web Pages can be:
Financial Data, News, Guides, Weather,
Legal Information, other..
A very important Web document or link is:
" The Future of Internet 2) a New
Technology and Standard for the Internet
under Development by the World Wide
Web Consortium (wwwc.) or W3C.

CHAPTER SEVEN
SIETE

THE INTERNET AND THE WORLD
WIDE WEB (WWW).

The Internet is the largest WAN (Wide
Area Network) in the world. The internet is
managed by the Internet Consortium
(ICANN) Internet Consortium for Assigned
Names and Numbers) and **ISO**
International Standard Organization, which
regulates standards and Protocols for the
Internet as well as policies. The internet
operates with Protocols and Standards that
are accepted worldwide.

Computers and Windows consist of three modes for their proper operation; Protocols, Standards and Policies.

Networks and the Internet Part One and Two. ___

Networks and the Internet are shown in Graphic format to illustrate the major parts of the configuration.

Internet Protocols. ___

Protocols are a set of Rules that tell the computer hardware and software how to behave and operate. The Internet uses Protocols to make connections on the Internet and networks, and to regulate the World Wide Web (WWW.)

The Internet Protocols are: http and https (hypertext transport protocol), and www. Or World Wide Web protocol, these protocols must be typed into another protocol called the URL or Universal Resource Locator.

The protocol is then displayed as:
http://www. Google.com
As an example.

The Internet Domain. ____

The Internet Domain is considered a major part of the Internet Network. The Internet Network is comprised of the Internet WAN and LAN. The WAN is the Wide Area Network and the LAN is the Local Area Network. Both networks use different types of equipment and Protocols.

The Internet Domain is managed by ICANN (Internet Corporation for Assigned Names and Numbers.) this is one of the organizations that Regulates the Internet, and assigns all of the top level domains that are used on the Internet.

The Domain Names or name, is stored in a Server called DNS or Domain Name Server. This type of High Level Computer is used to translate Domain Names into IP Addresses.

For example; an IP Address that is: 198.80.146.30 once translated by the DNS, becomes the Domain Name: **www.nmsu.edu as an example.**

The Web address and Web Page of an Internet site would be written as: **http://www.nmsu.edu/careers/index.html** Where, http:// is the Protocol, the Domain name is, **www.nmsu.edu** the Path is careers and index.html is the Web Page Name.

The Internet was developed in 1960 and the World Wide Web (www.) in 1990.
The Internet is identified as: " A World Wide Collection of Electronic Documents called a Web Page.
A " Web Browser" is the Application Software to access " Web Pages".

The Top Level Domains used on the Internet are:
.COM, .EDU, .BIZ, .INFO, .GOV, .MIL, .NAME, .PRO, .NET, .ORG, .AERO, and .COOP

Using the Internet. _____

To use the Internet, computers require a Web Application called a "Browser" such as IE Internet Explorer, or Firefox. They are several Browsers available for use on the Internet. The most popular ones are, Internet Explorer, Firefox, Opera, Safari, etc.. A **Web Page** is created for each Web Application, for example; you can use Firefox as your Web Browser with Google as your Web Page.

The Internet begins by starting a service called " Internet Service," when Windows 7 or 8 start up., then running the Application software or Browser, to allow the user to view Web Sites on the World Wide Web and their respective Web Pages. A very popular Web Browser is IE or Internet Explorer developed by Microsoft., other popular Web Browsers are Firefox, developed by Mozilla and Safari developed by Apple Computers. Other Web Browsers are available on the Internet, and can be downloaded for free.

Each Web Page address will be displayed in the Web address URL (Universal Resource Locator) window.

In this window is where the Protocol HTTP: or HTTPS: should be typed, followed by the symbol // and the words: WWW. (World Wide Web) followed by the Internet address; for example:

http://www.nmsu.edu/index.html

The http is the Protocol, which stands for: Hypertext Transport Protocol, and www. Is also a Protocol that identifies the world wide web. The **www.nmsu.edu** is called the " Domain" and index.html displays the Web Page Name. All Web Pages are displayed by their Index, and html (Hypertext Markup Language) is the Computer Language used to develop the index and Web Pages.

Some Web Pages are also developed using another language called XML (Extensible Markup Language).

Free Web Browser Plug-Ins._____

To extend the capability of your Web Browser, you may install one or more " Plug-Ins " that will enhance the display of Multimedia Elements on the Web Page you are viewing. Some of the Free Plug-Ins available on the Internet for downloading are the following: Acrobat Reader, to view

.pdf files on the Internet, or secure documents created with Acrobat in .pdf file format. FlashPlayer, from Macromedia.com, to view Graphic Animation on the Internet. , LiquidPlayer from liquidaudio.com to play Audio CD and MP3 audio files, RealOnePlayer, from Real.com to play and view live audio and video on the internet., Quicktime, from Apple.com to play HD Music audio and video on the Internet.; ShockwavePlayer, from Macromedia.com to play and view Multimedia 3D Graphics with HD audio and video, supporting Dolby 6.1 or higher and Surround Sound Formats.

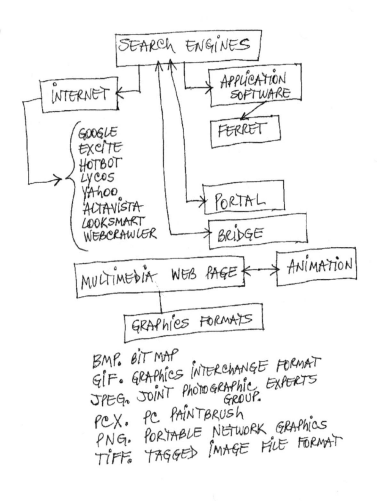

BMP. BIT MAP
GIF. GRAPHICS INTERCHANGE FORMAT
JPEG. JOINT PHOTOGRAPHIC EXPERTS
GROUP.
PCX. PC PAINTBRUSH
PNG. PORTABLE NETWORK GRAPHICS
TIFF. TAGGED IMAGE FILE FORMAT

Important Search Engines Graphics. __

Important Search Engines. ___

The software program contained in most Web Pages all have built in " Search Engines". The search engines are necessary for the user to be able to find what he or she is looking for. Some search engines will use the IP address or Internet Protocol Address, to search Web Sites and or Web Pages to find the information requested. Some Web Pages may contain one or more Search Engines.

Semantic Search Engines. ____

The following are very important search engines on the Internet: HotBot.com, Excite.com, AlltheWeb.com, Altavista.com, AskJeeves.com, Lycos.com, LookSmart.com, Webcrawler.com, Overture.com, Infospace.com, etc…

Graphic Formats used on the Internet. ____

The following Graphic Formats are used on the **WWW**. And are: **.png** (Portable Network Graphics); **.gif** (Graphic Interchange Format); **.bmp** (Bitmap); **.pcx** (PC Paintbrush); **.jpeg** (Joint Photographic Experts Group); **.tiff** (Tagged Image File Format).

Internet Protocol Address (IP.) uses the form: 198.80.146.30 or for example: 207.46.197.113 Which is equal to Microsoft Address: **www.microsoft.com** 207.46.197 identifies the Internet Network, and 113 identifies the Computer.

INTERNET WEB ADDRESSES vs. EMAIL ADDRESSES. __

Web addresses are different from Email addresses as they must contain the full Web Protocol, and is displayed as: **http://www.nmsu.edu** Email addresses are different as they only display the user name and At sign or @ with the ISP (Internet Service Provider) and is displayed as: johndoe@ yahoo.com or **marydoe@hotmail.com**

Standards.__

Standards are required on the Internet and all Computer Hardware and Software. The responsibility on these standards falls on an organization called **ISO** or International Standards Organization. This organization makes, changes, creates and modifies all standards for hardware and software. Standards are then divided into Proprietary, Defacto, National and International Standards, etc.. Some standards are open and accepted worldwide and becomes " defacto standards", such as HP standards for their Printers and other devices, and are HPGL (Hewlett Packard Graphic Language), PDL, Postscript Description Language, PDF Postscript Description File, etc..

Policies.___

Policies govern both hardware and software. Computer policies let the user's change the way computers behave and allow the users to modify the computer hardware to provide security on their system. An example is the Group Policy Editor or (GPEDIT.msc) a Microsoft Policy Editor and (SECPOL. msc) a Security Policy to set up your computer.

The Microsoft Management Console

.__ The Microsoft Management Console or **MMC** is built into every computer running Windows, and provides policies and rules and regulations that are user friendly and allows the users to modify and change how some parts of their computers should operate, by turning on and or shutting down services that are not needed or required in Windows OS. To see the available policies and other software, type into the search area by the start button, the command: MMC to bring up the Microsoft Management Console. The MMC allows the user to create **SNAPINS**, small utility programs that allow the user to manage, clean and secure his computer. Many SNAPINS are already included in the MMC to use right away.

After typing MMC into the Start or Run window on the lower left side of the computer desktop, the MMC Console window will be displayed, just select " add or remove snapins" to view and or select the snapin you want to work with, or use the following step by step procedure:

The Microsoft Management Console (MMC) let users create much more flexible user interfaces and customize administration tools.

MMC unifies and simplifies day-to-day system management tasks. It hosts tools and displays them as consoles. These tools, consisting of one or more applications, are built with modules called snap-ins. The snap-ins also can include additional extension snap-ins. MMC is a core part of Microsoft's management strategy and is included in Microsoft Windows® operating systems. In addition, Microsoft development groups will use MMC for future management applications.

Microsoft Management Console enables system administrators and users to create special tools to delegate specific administrative tasks to users or groups. Microsoft provides standard tools with the operating system that perform everyday administrative tasks that users need to accomplish. These are part of the All Users profile of the computer and located in the Administrative Tools group on the Startup menu. Saved as MMC console (.msc) files, these custom tools can be sent by e-mail, shared in a network folder, or posted on the Web. They can also be assigned to users, groups, or computers with system policy settings. A tool can be scaled up and down, integrated seamlessly into the operating system, repackaged, and customized.

Using MMC, system administrators can create unique consoles for workers who report to them or for workgroup managers. They can assign a tool with a system policy, deliver the file by e-mail, or post the file to a shared location on the network. When a workgroup manager opens the .msc file, access will be restricted to those tools provided by the system administrator.

Building your own tools with the standard user interface in MMC is a straightforward process. Start with an existing console and modify or add components to fulfill your needs. Or create an entirely new console. The following example shows how to create a new console and arrange its administrative components into separate windows.

Prerequisites and Requirements

There are no prerequisites: you don't need to complete any other step-by-step guide before starting this guide. You need one computer running either Windows 2000, Windows XP, Windows 7 or Windows 8. For the most current information about hardware requirements and compatibility for servers, clients, and peripherals, see the Check Hardware and

Software Compatibility page on the Windows website.

Creating Consoles

The most common way for administrators to use MMC is to simply start a predefined console file from the Start menu. However, to get an idea of the flexibility of MMC, it is useful to create a console file from scratch. It is also useful to create a console file from scratch when using the new task delegation features in this version of MMC.

Creating a New Console File **(SNAP-IN)**

1. On the Start Menu, click Run, type MMC, and then click OK. Microsoft Management Console opens with an empty console (or administrative tool) as shown in Figure 1 below. The empty console has no management functionality until you add some snap-ins. The MMC menu commands on the menu bar at the top of the Microsoft Management Console window apply to the entire console.

Figure 1: Beginning Console Window

2. Click Console (under Console1). On the Console Menu, click Add/Remove Snap-in. The Add/Remove Snap-in dialog box opens. This lets you enable extensions and configure which snap-ins are in the console file. You can specify where the snap-ins should be inserted in the Snap-in's "added to drop-down box." Accept the default, Console Root, for this exercise.

3. Click Add. This displays the Add Standalone Snap-in dialog box that lists the snap-ins that are installed on your computer.

4. From the list of snap-ins, double-click Computer Management to open the Computer Management wizard.

5. Click Local computer and select the check box for "Allow the selected computer to be changed when launching from the command line."

6. Click Finish. This returns you to the Add/Remove Snap-ins dialog box. Click Close.

7. Click the Extensions tab as shown in Figure 2 below. By selecting the check box Add all extensions, all locally-installed extensions on the computer are used. If this check box is not selected, then any extension snap-in that is selected is explicitly loaded when the console file is opened on a different computer.

Figure 2: Select All Extensions

8. Click OK to close the Add/Remove Snap-in dialog box. The Console Root window now has a snap-in, Computer Management, rooted at the Console Root folder.

Customizing the Display of <u>Snap-ins in the Console</u>: New Windows

After you add the snap-ins, you can add windows to provide different administrative views in the console.

To add windows

- In the left pane of the tree view in Figure 3 below, click the + next to Computer Management. Click System Tools.

Figure 3: Console1: System Tools

- Right-click the Event Viewer folder that opens, and then click New window from here. As shown in Figure 4 below, this opens a new Event Viewer window rooted at the

Event Viewer extension to computer management.

Figure 4: Event Viewer

- Click Window and click Console Root.
- In the Console Root window, click Services and Applications, right-click Services in the left pane, and then click New Window. As shown in Figure 5 below, this opens a new Services window rooted at the Event Viewer extension to Computer Management. In the new window, click the Show/Hide Console Tree toolbar button to hide the console tree, as shown in the red circle in Figure 5 below.

Figure 5: Show/Hide Button

- Close the original window with Console Root showing in it.

- On the Window menu, select Tile Horizontally. The console file should appear and include the information shown in Figure 4 and Figure 5 above.
- You can now save your new MMC console. Click the Save as icon on the Console window, and give your console a name. Your console is now saved as a .msc file, and you can provide it to anyone who needs to configure a computer with these tools.

Note: Each of the two smaller windows has a toolbar with buttons and drop-down menus. The toolbar buttons and drop-down menus on these each of these two windows apply only to the contents of the window. You can see that a window's toolbar buttons and menus change depending on the snap-in selected in the left pane of the window. If you select the View menu, you can see a list of available toolbars.

Tip: The windows fit better if your monitor display is set to a higher resolution and small font.

Creating Console Taskpads

If you are creating a console file for another user, it's useful to provide a very simplified view with only a few tasks available. Console taskpads help you to do this.

To create a console taskpad

- From the Window menu, select New Window. Close the other two windows (you will save a new console file at the end of this procedure). Maximize the remaining window.
- In the left pane, click the + next to the Computer Management folder, then click the + next to the System Tools folder. Click System, click the Event Viewer folder, right-click System, and select New Taskpad View.
- Go through the wizard accepting all the default settings. Verify the checkbox on the last page is checked so that the Task Creation wizard can start automatically.
- Choose the defaults in the Task Creation wizard until you come to the page shown below in Figure 6, then choose a list view task and select Properties:

Figure 6: New Task Wizard

- Click Next and accept the defaults for the rest of the screens. By selecting an Event and clicking Properties, you can see the property page for that Event.

After you click Finish on the last screen, your console should look like Figure 7 below:

Figure 7: New Console Showing System Event Log

- Click the Show/Hide console tree toolbar button.
- From the view menu, click Customize and click each of the options except the Description bar to hide each type of toolbar.

The next section discusses how to lock the console file down so that the user sees only a limited view. For right now your console file should look like Figure 8 below.

Figure 8: Customized View

Setting Console File Options

If you are creating a console file for another user, it is useful to prevent that user from further customizing the console file. The Options dialog box allows you to do this.

To set console file options

- From the Console menu, select Options.
- Change the Console Mode by selecting User Mode limited access, single window from the drop-down dialog box. This will prevent a user from adding new snap-ins to the console file or rearranging the windows.
- You can change the name from Console1. Click OK to continue.
- Save the console file. The changes will not take effect until the console file is opened again.

This is just one example of how the Microsoft Management Console lets you group information and functionality that previously would have required opening a Control Panel option plus two separate administrative tools. The modular architecture of MMC makes it easy for users to create snap-in Applications that leverage the platform while easing administrative load.

Built In MMC Snap-Ins. __

Microsoft has based most of its management applications on the Microsoft Management Console (MMC). The MMC provides a framework for building management consoles. Microsoft and many third-party application vendors have used this framework for creating their management consoles.

The MMC uses snap-ins for system and application management. Windows 7 & 8 comes with many built-in MMC snap-ins you can use to manage the system. You can use them to manage user settings, Windows applications, security, and many other vital aspects of the system.

Windows 7 & 8 contains the following built-in **MMC** snap-ins:

1ActiveX Control – You can add individual ActiveX controls to view and configure. These Internet Explorer plug-ins add functionality to the browser.

2Authorization Manager – You can set permissions for Authorization Manager-enabled applications.

3Certificates – You can configure different certificate stores available on the system. Certificates help provide a secure operating environment. You can use them for identification, securing data and securing communications. There are certificate stores for users, applications, and the system itself.

4Component Services – You can manage the system's COM+, or Component Services configuration. You can also configure Distributed Computer Object Model (DCOM) and Distributed Transaction Coordinator (DTC) settings. These are especially important when programs need to communicate between multiple computers.

5Computer Management – This is actually a collection of snap-ins used for task scheduling, disk management, performance monitoring, and many other configuration and management tasks.

6Device Manager – This is for viewing and configuring hardware installed on the system. You can disable devices, update drivers and troubleshoot potential issues.

7Disk Management – This is for disk and volume management. You can create volumes, format disks and enable fault tolerance.

8Event Viewer – This is for viewing system event logs that help you determine if your system or applications are having problems. You can also use the Security log to determine if there has been unauthorized access.

9Folder – This is to add a folder for organizing your snap-ins, which comes in handy if you've added numerous snap-ins to a single MMC console.

10Group Policy Object Editor – This lets you configure the Group Policy Objects on the system.

11IP Security Monitor – This helps you monitor the status of your IP Security (IPsec) configuration, which secures communication between computers.

12IP Security Policy Management – This helps you understand and configure the settings in your IPsec policy.

13Link to Web Address – This lets you add a Web page to the MMC, which can be useful for applications and systems with Web-based management.

14Local Users and Groups – This lets you configure users and groups on the local system, add user accounts, delete user accounts and configure various user properties.

15NAP Client Configuration – This lets you configure Network Access Protection (NAP) client configuration settings.

16Performance Monitor – This lets you monitor your system performance, including memory, hard disks, processors and a number of other components.

17Print Management – This helps you manage print servers and printers connected to the system.

18Resultant Set of Policy – This shows you what settings will be applied by your Group Policy settings, without actually applying them to the system.

19Security Configuration and Analysis – This analyzes your configuration and security templates.

20Security Templates – This lets you edit the security templates you applied to your system.

21Services – This lets you view and configure properties for services running on the system. You can disable, start, stop or restart services; configure authentication and fault tolerance.

22Shared Folders – This lets you view properties and status information for file shares. You can see what folders are being shared and who's accessing them.

23Task Scheduler – This lets you schedule tasks to be automatically run at specified times or at specified intervals.

24TPM Management – This lets you configure the Trusted Platform Module, which generates keys for cryptographic operations.

25Windows Firewall with Advanced Security –
This lets you configure Windows Firewall settings
to control what processes, applications, and
systems can access your system or generate
network traffic from your system.

26WMI Control – This lets you configure and
manage the Windows Management
Instrumentation (WMI) service, for managing and
monitoring Windows systems.

CHAPTER EIGHT
OCHO

Application Software and Support Tools.

Several Application Software and Support tools
are available to the user. Most of these tools are
built into the applications and or Windows
Operating Systems (OS) and are: Online Help,
User Manual, Web Based Help, Wizards, such as
the Memo Wizard; and Links to Websites that
contain FAQ (Frequently Asked Questions and
Chat Rooms.

Most Windows applications may contain support tools for Digital Video and Windows Movie Maker as well as tools to show audio and video compressed and stored files, and allow the user to choose Codec and to transfer Video from a Camera.

The following file formats are chosen sometimes by the System automatically or by the user: Apple Quicktime Formats (.mov and .qt); Microsoft Windows Media Player (.wmv and .asf); RealNetworks Realmedia (.rm and .ram). These formats are used by the application or the user to Encode Audio and Video.

The seven Pillars of Software Applications. ___

Seven Software steps exist to guide the user through the process of setting up any software.

The software process starts first with the " Setup and Install of the Application itself"., The User Install and the System Install, then we have the "Uninstall and Undelete" and the " Add and Remove", then the " Run and Delete", " The Free and Trial " and the " Open Source and Public Domain".

Software is divided into: Freeware Software, Trialware Software, Open Source Software and Public Domain Software.
All of these different types of Software can be obtained Free.
These types of Software are available for download from the Internet for free.

Multimedia Software and Applications. __

Many types of Multimedia and Windows Software Applications exist, the most important ones are: Printing Applications, Game Applications, Word Processing Applications, Microsoft Office Applications, Multimedia Applications, Drawing and Painting Applications, Network Applications. Under Word Processing Applications we have " Microsoft Word", Notepad and Word Pad to help the user write a simple letter or a more professional letter. Under Office Applications we have " Microsoft Office" and the Free Office Application " Open Office". Under Drawing and Painting Applications, we have Paint, Adobe Illustrator, Adobe Photoshop, Adobe Premier, and Adobe Acrobat. Under Network Applications, we have Port Scanner, and Network Monitor. Under Multimedia Applications, we have Windows Media Player, with CD/DVD Burner Software and Nero Software, that also read and burn CD's and Dvd's.

Windows Software Organization. __

Windows Software is organized into the following types of Software: Antivirus, Development, Lan, Games, Graphics, Wan, Cloud, Communications, Accessories, Utilities, Applications, Productivity, Multimedia, Programming, Basic, Paint, Web, Maintenance, Network, System, Server, Educational, Virtual, Hyper-V, Windows OS, Firewall, Security, Printer, and Email.

All of these Software types can be Installed, Deleted, Removed, Purged, Uninstalled, Undeleted, Shredded, and Destroyed.
The software can also be Shared, Open Source, Free, Public Domain, License, Encrypted, Decrypted, and Cypher protected.

Two special Software Tests are used: The Network Card or Adapter Test, and the DSL Router Test.
The Network Adapter Card Test is called the " loopback test" and it is performed by the user. Use the command " Ping" with **127.0.0.1** typed into the Command Line CMD. (ping 127.0.0.1) On the Computer, or just type it into the "start" window, on the lower left side of the Computer.

The DSL Router Test is done the same way, but using the address: 192.168.0.1 or 192.168.1.1 typed into the URL window of the Web Page that is been used on the Internet. Can be IE (Internet Explorer) or Firefox.

Software is developed from different computer languages, which are: HyperText, Basic, ADA, Unix, C and C++, Html, Xml, Low Level Languages like Fortran, Pascal, Cobol, and or High Level Compilers, like C and C++.

Software Standards. __

Software Standards are regulated by ISO International Standards Organization, IEEE (Project 802.x), Defacto, Network (OSI Model), and others.

When Software Applications do not work.__

In the case of Antivirus Application Software, the Antivirus Software can be Free or Licensed. The Software need to be Updated periodically by using " Update Now" or "Live Update" to update the " Virus Definition" File. If this file is not updated to the current definitions, the Software will not work. The Virus Definition, updates itself with the latest Viruses reported and any new Virus that is reported in the community.

CHAPTER NINE
NUEVE

Creating the " All Applications Folder". __

The All Applications Folder is created by the user, on the Computer Desktop. Right Click on any part of the Desktop and select New, and " Shortcut" from the menu. When the shortcut window is displayed, type in the location of the item: Explorer Shell:AppsFolder and click Next to continue.

Type the name of this shortcut, for example: ALL APPLICATIONS, and click Finish to create the shortcut as displayed below.

You may call this folder by any name you prefer, however the purpose will be to have a single folder on the desktop that contains all of the installed applications on the computer, regardless of their location in the All Programs section of the Windows system.

The All Applications folder will be created. This folder will look different from any other folder on the desktop. An example is displayed below.

All
Applications

Create Shortcut

What item would you like to create a shortcut for?

This wizard helps you to create shortcuts to local or network programs, files, folders, computers, or Internet addresses.

Type the location of the item:

Explorer Shell:AppsFolder

Browse...

Click Next to continue.

Next   Cancel

Name the ShortCut, and click Finish, to create the
Special Folder.

The All Applications folder will contain all of the
applications installed on the computer, more than
what is displayed in the Computer. You will be
able to see and display more than 166 items
installed on the computer by the system and
those installed by the user.

The advantage is that all those applications will
be able to launch immediately, bypassing the all
programs section of the computer.

They will launch very fast and will not require any "loading" by the system.

Creating the " Advantage" or Magic Folder. __

The Advantage folder is a very unique folder that can be created on the desktop. It requires typing an exact code after creating a New Folder on the desktop.
It is very important to remember to put a Period after the new folder is given a name, which can be " Magic." or "Advantage." or any name the user prefers, that identifies the content of the folder.

The folder will contain a tabulated and very organized list of over 200 items that covers every section of the Computer and how to troubleshoot that section and or specific instructions on what to do to fix the problem or problems you may encounter.

Start by creating a new folder on the desktop.
Right click and select New from the Menu to
create a New Folder. The New Folder will be
created. Give the New Folder a name, for
example: Magic. Or Advantage.
For example: Advantage.{ (open bracket) type in
Code….. (close bracket} then press <Enter> and
the New Advantage Folder will be created.

This folder will look completely different from
any other folder on the desktop including the All
applications folder.

Once the folder is created, you may double click
on it to open the folder and display all of the
tabulated files and menu's.
Enter the following Code exactly with the period
after the folder and dashes after the numbers,
after you name the folder:

**Advantage.{ED7BA470-8E54-465E-825C-
99712043E01C}** press Enter.
The Advantage folder will be created. See
examples below.

The Advantage Folder Created, will look like this:

These are some of the Files in the Advantage
folder:
Notice that they are Tabulated by sections in the
computer and the folder contains 256 items...
Each section like the "Action Center" displayed;
contains 18 different items that you can do and or
troubleshoot in this section. Other sections of the
computer will contain more items.

This unique folder will contain information and instructions on how to Navigate your Computer in Windows 7 or 8, and how to perform Diagnostics on your computer, the use of Quick Access Menus, How to boot into Safe Mode, how to install Plug Ins on your computer, monitoring your computer temperature, using a Word processor, using Narrator to read your documents,using Microsoft Office Applications, saving your work files, using paint applications, how to Calibrate your computer colors, setting up your Email, using Multimedia Applications, using the Internet, how to monitor and test your network and adapter cards, how to setup your wireless network, and how to clean and protect your computer with utilities., and many more items.

Use a Flashdrive as Memory with Ready Boost. __

Ready Boost will work better on Computers with low RAM or Memory, from 2 GB, to 4 GB. Aprox. Ready Boost is built into every computer running Windows 8 operating System. To access Ready Boost, go to Computer or My Computer and select your Flashdrive that you just connected to your USB port. You may use any USB Port on your computer.

The Flashdrive that will be used should be at least 4 Gb Gigabytes or higher. Eight (8) Gigabytes capacity is preferred. Only 4094 Bytes   (4 GB minimum) is recommended to dedicate for Ready Boost.

Once you select your Flashdrive, right click it to select Properties.
Select the Ready Boost Tab
Check" Dedicate this device to Ready Boost"
Select the " space to reserve for system speed"
Windows recommends reserving 4094 Bytes for best results;
Click on Apply, then <ok>
Restart the Computer.
Your Flashdrive will now be dedicated with Ready Boost as more additional memory, and the computer should run faster.

Using the Built in Diagnostics for your Computer. ___

A complete set of Diagnostics Tools are built into Windows for the user to troubleshoot, as well as other hidden tools.
To use the built in Diagnostics, type into the search box on the lower left corner of the desktop, the words: **DXDiag**
This will bring up the Direct X Diagnostic Tool. With four Tabs, System, Display, Sound and Input. This will give the user a Report of each of these sections on the computer and note if any problems are found or detected.

It is a good idea to run this tool periodically if you suspect that the Computer is not working correctly. This is a tool the user can access at any time.

The Quick Access Menu Tool. ____

The Quick Access menu Tool is one of the other tools available to the user. To access this tool, hold down the " **Windows Key"** on your Keyboard and **press the X key.** This key is located on the lower left side of the keyboard, beside the ALT key and has a Symbol of a Flag on top of it.

The Quick Access menu will Display 16 Items to allow the user to navigate to these sections of the computer very quickly.

The Defragment and Optimize Drive Tool.

—

This built-in tool allow the user to Defragment the drives on the computer and Optimize the drives as well.

To access this tool, just type into the search window on the lower left side of the computer, the words: **DEFR** and the Defragment window will be displayed. Select the " Defragment Drives and Optimize".

You may set the tool to Optimize the Drives on the computer automatically when the Tool is displayed. The tool will show the drives on the computer and their status. The drives will be analyzed first before they are optimized.

The Calibrate your Screen Tool. ___

The Windows built-in Calibrate Tool allows the user to calibrate the Computer Screen. To access the tool just type into the Search box on the lower left side of the computer the words: DCCW

The Display Color Calibration Window will be displayed.
Just follow the instructions.

The Shutdown Tool in Windows 8. ___

One of the other built in tools available to the user is the " Shutdown Tool" in Windows 8. This Tool provides a correct and alternate way to properly shutdown the computer.

To access this tool, hold down the ALT key and press the F4 function Key, located on the first row of the keyboard.

This will display the shutdown window, that is displayed below:

Windows can also be shutdown using the Windows Shutdown utility called" **Slide to Shutdown.exe"** this file is located on the computer in   **C:/windows/system32** on the Hard Drive.

The Windows shutdown window will allow the user to shutdown correctly and quickly as well as other things by selecting the arrow in the shutdown window. To Shutdown Windows, just click on OK.

WINDOWS 8 HOTKEYS. ___

1. Win key - Toggles between Start Screen and Windows Desktop

2. Win+X - Opens Quick Access Menu as mentioned in point 1

3. Win+PrntScr - Automatically saves screenshot in Pictures folder as mentioned in point 2

4. Win+C - Shows Charms Bar

5. Win+I - Shows Settings panel

6. Win+K - Launches Devices charm

7. Win+H - Launches Share charm

8. Win+Q - Launches Search charm

9. Win+W - Launches Settings search page

10. Win+F - Launches Files search page

11. Win+Tab - Shows Metro apps switcher as mentioned in point 4

12. Win+Z - Shows / hides App bar at Start Screen to show all apps

13. Win+Spacebar - Toggles between input languages and keyboard layout

14. Win+, - From Start Screen peeks at the Desktop

15. Win+Enter - Launches Narrator

16. Ctrl+F1 - Minimizes / maximizes ribbon in Windows Explorer

17. Ctrl+Tab – Launches All Apps list on Start Screen

18. Ctrl+Shift+N- To create a New Folder quickly

The following Graphics below depict where to go to get the Software to keep your Computer Clean of Malware and other types of Viruses that can harm your computer.

How to keep your Computer Clean. __

How to keep your Computer Clean from Malware and other programs that may harm the Computer. Also, where to go and find Free Software and Utilities on the Internet.

What Computers Can do and Can Not do.

UNDERSTANDING

WHAT COMPUTERS <u>CAN</u> AND <u>CAN NOT</u> DO.

1. Basic Computers **cannot**, and **<u>are not:</u>**

a. Dumb Terminals

b. Only Game machines

c. Just Hardware

d. Just Software

e. Cannot divide by Zero (0)

f. Empty boxes with Input and Output

g. Immune to Sickness or Infections

h. Will not last forever

i. Have a shelf-life

j. Secure all the time

COMPUTERS <u>ARE</u> AND <u>CAN.</u>

a. Task driven Machines

b. Analytical

c. Are Intelligent

d. Use their own Language (Binary)

e. Understands English and other Languages

f. Universal Machines

g. Have Memory

h Remembers

i. Can be self-healing

j. Can Teach itself

k. First Line of Defense (Access, Rights, Privilege, Permissions)

l. Part of The Grid

m. Fast efficient when used correctly

n. Consults with Mom and Dad

o. Have SPI's to Report and Communicate

p. Have SPO's to Communicate and Report

q. Can Talk, Speak, Read in several Languages

r. Can give Access, Rights, Privileges and Permissions

s. Have a **Universal Password** (*Axxx*)

t. Have a **Universal User** (*Hxxxx)*

u. Are Secure Machines with proper Software or Policies

v. Have Lock and Key

w. Have Encryption (Bitlocker)

x. Use Protocols to communicate

y. Use Standards

z. Can Lock You Out

aa. Talk to Satellites (GPS)

bb. Can be Wireless

cc. Can find you

dd. Knows where you are

ee. Can see you

ff. Can Read and Write to you

gg. Send your Mail and Receive Mail

hh. Can Play

ii. Can become Super-Computers

jj. Are used by all ages

kk. Are Multi-Lingual

ll. Are Teaching Machines

mm. Have a Heart (The CPU)

nn. Think Faster

oo. Get Sick with Viruses

pp. Can be Inoculated

qq. Are User Friendly

rr. Other duties as assigned.

CHAPTER TEN
DIEZ

Basic Computer Terms

CPU
> *Central processing unit*; the brain of the computer; controls the other elements of the computer

Disk Drive
> A peripheral device that reads and/or writes information on a disk

Hard Drive
> A device (usually within the computer case) that reads and writes information, including the operating system, program files, and data files

Keyboard
> A peripheral used to input data by pressing keys

Modem
> A peripheral device used to connect one computer to another over a phone line

Monitor

A device used to display information visually

Mouse

A peripheral device used to point to items on a monitor

NIC

Network interface card; a board inserted in a computer that provides a physical connection to a network

Printer

A peripheral device that converts output from a computer into a printed image

Software

Applications

Complete, self-contained programs that perform a specific function (ie. spreadsheets, databases)

Bit

A computer's most basic unit of information that represents zero (0) or one (1)

Boot

The process of loading or initializing an operating system on a computer; usually occurs as soon as a computer is turned on

Browser

A program used to view World Wide Web pages, such as Netscape Navigator or Internet Explorer

Bug

A part of a program that usually causes the computer to malfunction; often remedied in patches or updates to the program

Byte

Small unit of data storage; 8 bits; usually holds one character, 8 bits equal 1 byte

Click

Occurs when a user presses a button on a mouse which in turn, generates a command to the computer

Database

A large structured set of data; a file that contains numerous records that contain numerous fields

Diskette

A small flexible disk used for storing computer data

Double Click

Occurs when a user presses a button on the mouse twice in quick succession; this generates a command to the computer

Download

Transferring data from another computer to your computer

Drag

Occurs when a user points the mouse at an icon or folder, presses the button and without releasing the button, moves the icon or folder to another place on the computer where the button is released

Driver

Software program that controls a piece of hardware or a peripheral

FAQ

Frequently asked question; documents that answer questions common to a particular website or program

File

Namable unit of data storage; an element of data storage; a single sequence of bytes

Folder

A graphical representation used to organize a collection of computer files; as in the concept of a filing cabinet (computer's hard drive) with files (folders)

Freeware

Software provided at no cost to the user

Gigabyte

1,073,741,824 bytes or 1,024 megabytes; generally abbreviated GB

GUI

Graphical user interface; uses pictures and words to represent ideas, choices, functions, etc.

Icon

A small picture used to represent a file or program in a GUI interface

Internet
> A network of computer networks encompassing the World Wide Web, FTP, telnet, and many other protocols

IP number
> *Internet protocol*; a computer's unique address or number on the Internet

Kilobyte
> 1,024 bytes; usually abbreviated KB

Megabyte
> 1,048,576 bytes or 1,024 kilobytes; enough storage to approximately equal a 600 page paperback book; generally abbreviated Mb

Memory
> Any device that holds computer data

Menu
> A list of operations available to the user of a program

Network
> A collection of computers that are connected

Peripheral
> Any of a number of hardware devices connected to a CPU

RAM
> *Random access memory*; the type of storage that changes; when the computer is turned off, the RAM memory is erased

ROM
> *Read-only memory*; the type of storage that is not changed even when the computer is turned off

Scroll Bar

Allows the user to control which portion of the document is visible in the window; available either horizontally or vertically or both

Shareware

Software provided at a minimal cost to users who are on their honor to send in payment to the programmer

Spreadsheet

A program arranged in rows and columns that manipulates numbers

Tool Bar

A graphical representation of program activities; a row of icons used to perform tasks in a program

URL

Universal or Uniform resource locator; the address of a site on the World Wide Web; a standard way of locating objects on the Internet

Virus

A deliberately harmful computer program designed to create annoying glitches or destroy data

Window

A screen in a software program that permits the user to view several programs at one time

Word Processor

A program that allows the user to create primarily text documents

Wi-Fi

Wireless Network standard 802.11 a/b/g/n for Wireless Network Adapters

Application Files
Program files environment where you can create and edit the kind of document that application makes.

Click
To select an object by pressing the mouse button when the cursor is pointing to the required menu option, icon or hypertext link.

Close
To close a window that has been opened for viewing and / or editing.

Computer
A general-purpose machine that processes data according to a set of instructions that are stored internally either temporarily or permanently.

Central Processor Unit (CPU)
This term has two meanings (just to confound beginners, you understand)
1) Central Processor Unit--the main chip on the computer that makes everything go.
2) The box that holds the guts of the computer.
A faster CPU is always better than a slower one. You can never have too fast of a CPU.

Crash
Your computer or application no longer works correctly and so you "loose" all the work you've done since the last time you saved.

Creating A File
Storing data as a file with an assigned file name that is unique within the directory it resides in.

Delete
To remove an item of data from a file or to remove a file from the disk.

Desktop
An on-screen representation of a desktop such as used in the Macintosh and Windows operating systems.

Dialog Boxes
Takes over your screen and allows you to "dialog" with the computer.

Directory (AKA Folder, sub-directory)
Allows you to organize files and other folders.

Disk Space
This is the place where your files live. The greater the disk space the more files you can keep. (See also Megabytes)
More disk space is always better than less. You can never have much disk space.

Documents
Files you create and edit.

Document Files
Files we care about (memos, letters, pictures, etc.)

Double Click
To press the mouse button twice in rapid succession without moving the mouse between clicks.

Drag
To move an object on screen in which its complete movement is visible from starting location to destination.

Edit
To make a change to existing data.

File Cabinet
Metaphorically, the hard drive (and other kinds of storage media like floppy disks) which store files and folders.

Folder (AKA Directory, Sub-Directory)
Allows you to organize files and other folders.

Folder Icons
Collections of documents and other folders.

Icons
In a graphical user interface (GUI), a small, pictorial, on screen representation of an object, such as a document, program, folder or disk drive.

Icon View
Allows you to see icons of folders and files primarily as icons with little information.

Keyboard
This if the primary text input device. It also contains certain standard function keys, such as the Escape key, tab, and arrow keys, shift and control keys, and sometimes other manufacturer-customized keys.

Kilo (K)
This is a unit of measure = 1,000. So 1,000 bytes is a KiloByte.

List View
Shows the icons but also orders the icons (often by name, but can sort the list in other ways) and shows more information about them.

Macintosh
The brand name of a family of personal computers (hardware) and an operating system (software) from Apple, introduced in 1984.

Megabytes (Mb)
Mega = million so Mb is 1,000,000 bytes. It's enough information for the computer to store one character (e.g. "h"), so 1mb text file = 1,000,000 keystrokes in that file. Just to confound the masses, although RAM and Disk Space do something completely different we measure both in megabytes. This leads to confusion.

MegaHertz (Mhz)
This stands for MegaHertz. A hertz is an electronics term. 1 hz = one cycle (or wavelength) per second. 1 megahertz = 1,000,000 cycles per second.
In computer jargon, Mhz measures how *fast* your CPU chip runs. Although it's more important to know the chip than the speed, if you're comparing the same kind of CPU chip then a higher / faster CPU speed (measured in MHz) is better than a slower speed.

Menu
Displays a list of commands, some with images next to them.

Modifier Keys
Keys that change the meaning of what you type.

Mouse
Pointing device that allows you to tell the computer what to do.

Operating System (OS)
System software that allows your computer to work.

Pointer (AKA Cursor)
The name of the arrow (or other shape) that tracks across the screen as you move the mouse (or other pointing device) around.

Random Access Memory (RAM)
This stands for Random Access Memory. You can think of this as the "space" where you computer does its processing. The more space you have the more processes you can run at the same time. More RAM is always better than less. You can never have much RAM.

Recycle Bin
Place where you put files and folders that you may later want to delete or get rid of. Compare Trash.

Resize Box
Allows you to change the size and shape of a window.

Right click
To press the right button on the mouse. (This is Windows specific. On a Mac running System 8 or higher, you hold down the Control key and then click to get the same effect.)

Save
Tell the computer to create a file on disk that has the

information you've put into the document (usually typing).

Save As
Give the file a name and/or store the file in a certain place.

Scroll bar
Allows you to move around through your document.

Shut down
To quit all applications and turn off the computer.

Software
Instructions that tell the computer what to do.

System files
Allows our computer to work.

Trash
Place where you put files and folders that you want to delete or get rid of.

Volume Icons
Devices that hold files and folders.

Windows
1) The most widely used operating system for personal computers from Microsoft. (Software only. Other companies manufacture the hardware that runs the Windows Operating System.) Compare Macintosh. (Windows with a large "W".)
2) The thing you see on screen that contains a directory listing or the contents of a document. (Window with a small "w".)

CHAPTER 11
ONCE

Application Software. ___

Application Software is divided into six different groups: (1) Package Software,(2) Custom Software,(3) Shareware(Trial) Software,(4) Software Suite,(5) Freeware Software,(6) and Public Domain Software (7).

System Software as well as Application Software is installed by the User. Some System software and some Application software operate directly on the Computer Hardware, for example the Windows OS 8. The other Application Software that is dependant on the hardware, fall into the following categories:
Spreadsheet, Database, Graphics, Project Management, Multimedia, Medical, Scientific, Travel, Video and Audio, Education, and Multimedia Entertainment.

Rules in Computing. ___

The Rule of 30. ____

To prevent "Eye Fatigue" if you have to work on your Computer for long hours, look at something that is approximately 30 feet away for 30 seconds every 30 minutes.

The First Rule of Protection for Computers.__

The first Rule is **ACCESS** , if you give anyone access to your Computer, it means that you have given them your Key.
Do not give anyone access to your Computer
Once access is obtained, the Computer becomes vulnerable.
Access can be Physical Access or Software Access.

The second Rule is: **PRIVILEGE** Once privilege is obtained; the computer, is exposed to any malware and or damage to critical components and critical parts of the Computer registry, affecting the Operating System.

The third Rule is **RIGHTS** if rights is obtained, then The User Computer can be Destroyed, and any or all parts of the computer hardware and software is compromised, and the user computer is attacked by malicious software.
Note: Microsoft have created a " Malicious Software Removal Tool"
To get rid of this type of attack on User's Computers. This Tool is Free and available to download at http:// **www.microsoft.com**

The fourth Rule is **PERMISSIONS** if an attacker get permission to access the User Computer, then he or she can Destroy or do anything they want to the user Computer and will have access to all the Security settings. The Computer is then considered lost and   un-recoverable.

An example of the above Rule is:
A father talking to his son " JOHN".
John, here are **the keys** to the new Mercedes, Gold Edition

You have access and can use the Radio and all the expensive electronics in the car and the built in Game system. You do not have the right to pick up any strangers or have any kind of alcohol beverages in the car.

You can drive around town, but you do not have permission to leave the State of New Mexico or to go more than 15 Miles in any direction.

Cleaning and Protecting the User Computer. ___

Software Utilities. ____

Software Utilities are small programs written to Clean the User Computer Registry and other parts of the Computer.

Some of these utilities are not Cleaners but work on other parts of the Computer Hardware and Software and are considered " Optimizers and or Tune Up Utilities.

The Registry is the most important part of the Computer, and keeping it clean and optimized will ensure that the user Computer will always be fast and productive.

The user computer hardware and software is always under attack by Viruses and Malicious Software, it is important therefore to keep the user computer clean and free from Viruses and or any attack that can harm the System.

The following is a list of Free Utilities designed to keep the Computer Clean, and Secured. These utilities do not take the place of the Application " Antivirus" which is a full Software program designed to "Protect" the user Computer from Viruses and have nothing to do with Cleaning or Tune-Up.

All user's Computers should have an Antivirus program, and one or more Registry Cleaner with a Malicious Removal Tool.

The Free Utilities are:
- Glary Utilities version **5.80**
- Advanced System Care **10.5**
- Acebyte Utilities 3.0.2
- Malawarebytes 2.0
- Clean Master
- Windows Malicious Removal Tool
- Windows utilities
- Apache Open Office 4.0.0 Win_x86

- AVG Free Antivirus_86_all_2017_4716a7754
- LibreOffice_4.2.5_Win_x86
- TuneUpUtilities 2017_en-US

All of these utilities are Free and available for Download on the Internet.

CHAPTER 12
DOCE

The Fixed and Wireless Printer. ___

Many different kind of printers are available, but they all have something in common., the Print Engine inside the hardware., also all printers must meet the same international standards established by ISO and also Defacto Standards.

One of the most popular printer and also developer of the Printer print Engine as well as many Defacto Standards is, HP or Hewlett Packard Company. The Standards developed by HP became very popular and was accepted as a "Defacto" standard, which means in simple terms a standard used and adopted, by everyone and available Free in some cases.

Printers developed by other companies local or international will use HP Print Engine as well as HP Defacto Standards. HP developed many years ago de following standards now adopted worldwide. HPGL Hewlett Packard Graphic Language, PDL Postscript Description Language, HPGPIB Hewlett Packard General Purpose Interface Bus, PDF Postscript Description File, etc.. These Standards are now used in every Printer.

In addition to the HP Print Engine, the other part of the Printer hardware that is very important is the Printer " Gamut".
The Printer Gamut is an Array of All possible Colors that can be printer and or Displayed. The printer Gamut determines the Printer Resolution and capability to display and Print Millions of Colors following the International Color Standards.

In the beginning we could only print and display limited colors, 4 to 8 colors only with the Standard; RGB Red, Green and Blue.

Later on, other color Standards were developed, such as: CMYK(0) or, Cyan, Magenta, Yellow and K which represents zero (0) or (1).

When the K bit or Pixel was turned on; the color was White, when it was off (0) the color was Black.

This Standard gave printers the capability to Print 64 Colors or more.

New Standards were developed, like CROMALIN from Dupont, and PANTONE Certified Colors, which allowed the display and printing of Thousands and Millions of colors and shades.

In the mean time, Computer Monitors were developed to use the same Standards to allow for the display of millions of colors to offer High Resolution for Graphics, Video and Multimedia displays.

These same standards are used on Television sets today to display HD High Definition Graphics, Sound and Video., and very High Definition Displays (1080P) measured in Pixels.

Printers must meet the Color Standards and should have a large GAMUT (64 Bit) or higher; to allow the Printer to Print High Resolution Text and Graphics in many colors.

The Printer Memory. _____

Most printers should have enough RAM Memory installed to store FONTS and other Graphic Software. Printers should have at least 4Gb of RAM Memory installed.

The Printer Ports. _____

Most Printers should have at least two (2) USB Ports. The Standard USB Port is USB 2.0, the New Standard for USB (Universal Serial Bus) is USB 3.0 which is much faster.
The USB Ports are used to connect the Printer to the Computer USB Port so that the User can Print to the Printer., it requires a USB Cable that is included in most printers.

The Wireless Printer and Standard._____

Most Printers today are built with Wireless capabilities, also called Wi-Fi. As with Computers, Wi-Fi is built into the computer hardware and contains an Adapter called a Wireless Network Adapter or Card.

This Wireless card is now built into every computer and Printer, to give the hardware wireless capabilities.

Wireless technology or Wi-Fi must meet the Wi-Fi Standard 802.11

That is defined as 802.11 a/b/g that originally only supported 54 Mbp and operated in 2.4 Mhz and 5.0 Mhz frequencies.

Later on a new standard 802.11 a/b/g/**n** was developed that increased the data rate to 100 Mbps and operated at higher frequencies.

The New Standard that was released last year is 802.11 a/b/g/n/**ac** and **ad**. This New Standard allows Wi-Fi to operate at very high Frequencies of 20 and 60 GHz. Increasing the data rate to Gigabit speeds and beyond.

Wi-Fi capable Printers are easy to use and setup, as no cables is required and the Printer is detected by the Network immediately as just another device. The built-in software will automatically setup the printer for the user.

WINDOWS SHORTCUTS. ___

1.   Press and Hold the Windows Key, then press "**T**" to access all Pinned Applications on bottom toolbar.

2.   Press and hold the Windows Key (**WinKey**) and press **R** to Open the **RUN** Dialog.

3.   **Shift + F8** to access " **SAFE MODE** " when Computer is booting up

4.   Open RUN Dialog and type : Shell:AppsFolder to access the " All Applications Folder" ..

5. Slide to Shutdown Windows Utility, located in C:/Windows/system32 on the Hard Drive

Windows System key combinations

- F1: Help
- CTRL+ESC: Open **Start** menu
- ALT+TAB: Switch between open programs
- ALT+F4: Quit program
- SHIFT+DELETE: Delete item permanently
- Windows (WinKey) Logo+L: Lock the computer (without using CTRL+ALT+DELETE)

Windows program key combinations

- CTRL+C: Copy
- CTRL+X: Cut
- CTRL+V: Paste
- CTRL+Z: Undo
- CTRL+B: Bold
- CTRL+U: Underline
- CTRL+I: Italic

Mouse click/keyboard modifier combinations for shell objects

1. SHIFT+right click: Displays a shortcut menu containing alternative commands

2.   SHIFT+double click: Runs the alternate default command (the second item on the menu)

3.   ALT+double click: Displays properties

4.   SHIFT+DELETE: Deletes an item immediately without placing it in the Recycle Bin

General keyboard-only commands

- F1: Starts Windows Help

- F10: Activates menu bar options

- SHIFT+F10 Opens a shortcut menu for the selected item (this is the same as right-clicking an object

- **CTRL+ESC: Opens the Start menu** (use the ARROW keys to select an item)

- CTRL+ESC or ESC: Selects the **Start** button (press TAB to select the taskbar, or press SHIFT+F10 for a context menu)

- **CTRL+SHIFT+ESC: Opens Windows Task Manager**

- ALT+DOWN ARROW: Opens a drop-down list box

- ALT+TAB: Switch to another running program (hold down the ALT key and then press the TAB key to view the task-switching window)

- SHIFT: Press and hold down the SHIFT key while you insert a CD-ROM to bypass the automatic-run feature
- **ALT+SPACE: Displays the main window's System menu** (from the System menu, you can restore, move, resize, minimize, maximize, or close the window)
- ALT+- (ALT+hyphen): Displays the Multiple Document Interface (MDI) child window's System menu (from the MDI child window's **System** menu, you can restore, move, resize, minimize, maximize, or close the child window)
- CTRL+TAB: Switch to the next child window of a Multiple Document Interface (MDI) program
- ALT+**underlined letter in menu**: Opens the menu
- ALT+F4: Closes the current window
- CTRL+F4: Closes the current Multiple Document Interface (MDI) window
- ALT+F6: Switch between multiple windows in the same program (for example, when the Notepad Find dialog box is displayed, ALT+F6 switches between the **Find** dialog box and the main Notepad window)

Shell objects and general folder/Windows Explorer shortcuts

For a selected object:

- F2: Rename object
- F3: Find all files
- CTRL+X: Cut
- CTRL+C: Copy
- CTRL+V: Paste
- **<u>SHIFT+DELETE: Delete selection immediately</u>**, without moving the item to the Recycle Bin
- ALT+ENTER: Open the properties for the selected object

To copy a file

Press and hold down the CTRL key while you drag the file to another folder.

To create a shortcut

<u>Press and hold down CTRL+SHIFT while you drag a file to the desktop or a folder.</u>

General folder/shortcut control

Appendix A: F4: Selects the **Go To A Different Folder** box and moves down the entries in the box (if the toolbar is active in Windows Explorer)

Appendix B: F5: Refreshes the current window.

Appendix C: F6: Moves among panes in Windows Explorer

Appendix D: CTRL+G: Opens the Go To Folder tool (in Windows 95 Windows Explorer only)

Appendix E: CTRL+Z: Undo the last command

Appendix F: CTRL+A: Select all the items in the current window

Appendix G: BACKSPACE: Switch to the parent folder

Appendix H: SHIFT+click+Close button: For folders, close the current folder plus all parent folders

Windows Explorer tree control

- Numeric Keypad *: Expands everything under the current selection
- Numeric Keypad +: Expands the current selection
- Numeric Keypad -: Collapses the current selection.
- RIGHT ARROW: Expands the current selection if it is not expanded, otherwise goes to the first child
- LEFT ARROW: Collapses the current selection if it is expanded, otherwise goes to the parent

Properties control

- CTRL+TAB/CTRL+SHIFT+TAB: Move through the property tabs

Accessibility shortcuts

- Press SHIFT five times: Toggles StickyKeys on and off
- Press down and hold the right SHIFT key for eight seconds: Toggles FilterKeys on and off
- Press down and hold the NUM LOCK key for five seconds: Toggles ToggleKeys on and off
- Left ALT+left SHIFT+NUM LOCK: Toggles MouseKeys on and off
- Left ALT+left SHIFT+PRINT SCREEN: Toggles high contrast on and off

Microsoft Natural Keyboard keys

1. Windows Logo: **Start** menu
2. **<u>Windows Logo+R: Run dialog box</u>**
3. Windows Logo+M: Minimize all
4. SHIFT+Windows Logo+M: Undo minimize all
5. Windows Logo+F1: Help
6. Windows Logo+E: Windows Explorer
7. Windows Logo+F: Find files or folders
8. Windows Logo+D: Minimizes all open windows and displays the desktop
9. CTRL+Windows Logo+F: Find computer

10. CTRL+Windows Logo+TAB: Moves focus from Start, to the Quick Launch toolbar, to the system tray (use RIGHT ARROW or LEFT ARROW to move focus to items on the Quick Launch toolbar and the system tray)

11. Windows Logo+TAB: Cycle through taskbar buttons

12. Windows Logo+Break: **System Properties** dialog box

13. Application key: Displays a shortcut menu for the selected item

Microsoft Natural Keyboard with IntelliType software installed

1) Windows Logo+L: Log off Windows

2) Windows Logo+P: Starts Print Manager

3) Windows Logo+C: Opens Control Panel

4) Windows Logo+V: Starts Clipboard

5) Windows Logo+K: Opens **Keyboard Properties** dialog box

6) Windows Logo+I: Opens **Mouse Properties** dialog box

7) Windows Logo+A: Starts Accessibility Options (if installed)

8) Windows Logo+SPACEBAR: Displays the list of Microsoft IntelliType shortcut keys

9) Windows Logo+S: Toggles CAPS LOCK on and off

Dialog box keyboard commands

- TAB: Move to the next control in the dialog box
- SHIFT+TAB: Move to the previous control in the dialog box
- SPACEBAR: If the current control is a button, this clicks the button. If the current control is a check box, this toggles the check box. If the current control is an option, this selects the option.
- ENTER: Equivalent to clicking the selected button (the button with the outline)
- ESC: Equivalent to clicking the **Cancel** button
- **ALT+underlined letter in dialog box item**: Move to the corresponding item

Computer Graphics depicting parts of this Book. _____

COMPUTER VIRUSSES. —

VIRUS

PROGRAM THAT SPREADS BY REPLICATING ITSELF INTO OTHER PROGRAMS.

WORM

SELF REPLICATING, BUT DOES NOT ATTACH ITSELF. A SELF CONTAINED PROGRAM.

TROJAN

PROGRAM APPEARS TO BE USEFUL BUT CONTAINS MALWARE, EJ. A UTILITY.

MALWARE

ANY SOFTWARE PROG. DESIGNED TO CAUSE HARM.

HOAX VIRUS

WORSE KIND OF VIRUS, SENDS HOAX MESSAGES TO USERS.

ROOT KITS

FORM OF TROJAN, MONITORS TRAFFIC TO AND FROM YOUR COMPUTER, AND ALTERS SYSTEM FILES.

SPYWARE

AFFECTS EMAIL, MONITORS AND CONTROL PART OF YOOR COMPUTER, DECREASE COMPUTER PETORMANCE

SPAM

A NUISANCE, NOT A THREAT, ITS UNSOLICIT MAIL (E-MAIL)   (ED)

ADAWARE

LIKE SPYWARE, AFFECTS COMPUTER PERFORMANCE

BASIC COMPUTER.—

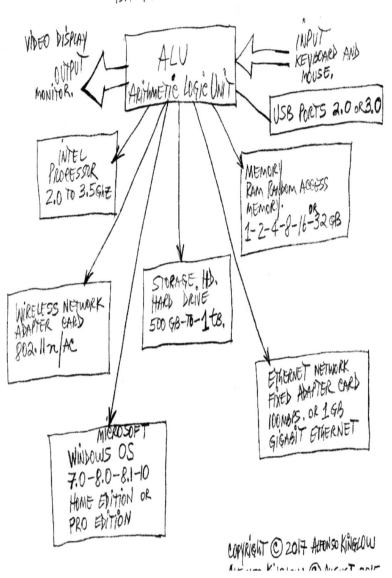

VIDEO DISPLAY
OUTPUT
monitor.

ALU
Arithmetic Logic Unit

INPUT
KEYBOARD AND
MOUSE.

USB PORTS 2.0 OR 3.0

INTEL
PROCESSOR
2.0 TO 3.5GHZ

MEMORY
RAM RANDOM ACCESS
MEMORY.
1-2-4-8-16-32 GB

WIRELESS NETWORK
ADAPTER CARD
802.11 n/AC

STORAGE. HD.
HARD DRIVE
500 GB TO 1 TB.

ETHERNET NETWORK
FIXED ADAPTER CARD
100Mbps. OR 1 GB
GIGABIT ETHERNET

MICROSOFT
WINDOWS OS
7.0-8.0-8.1-10
HOME EDITION OR
PRO EDITION

MACHINE AND HUMAN BASIC INFORMATION PROCESS.—

COMPUTER ⟸= A TASK DRIVEN MACHINE

OTHER
FLASH DRIVE
DISK
VIDEO DISPLAY ⟶ OUTPUT ⟸ ALU ⟸ INPUT
TAPE RECORDER
MONITOR

KEYBOARD
MOUSE
TAPE
MICROPHONE
OTHER

OS   RAM   ROM   PROM

DAD   CPU   MOM

BASIC INFORMATION

MACHINE PROCESS

SPI's   ANALITICAL   STATISTICAL   SPO's
RULES   DATA   DATA   PURE
         LAWS   MATHEMATICS

EMPIRICAL   NUMBERS
IMAGINARY
STANDARDS &
PROTOCOLS
ANALOG & DIGITAL

HUMAN PROCESS

CRITICAL   CONDITIONAL   LOGICAL   ANALITICAL
THINKING   THINKING   THINKING   THINKING

MULTITASKING   COMPARATIVE
                THINKING

2017 COPYRIGHT © A. KINGLOW

COPYWRITE © ALFONSO KINGLOW 5/17

MACHINE AND HUMAN BASIC INFORMATION PROCESS.—

COMPUTER ⇐ A TASK DRIVEN MACHINE

OTHER
FLASH DRIVE
DISK
VIDEO DISPLAY
TAPE RECORDER
MONITOR
OUTPUT ⇐ ALU ⇐ INPUT

KEYBOARD
MOUSE
TAPE
MICROPHONE
OTHER

OS RAM ROM PROM
DAD CPU MOM

BASIC INFORMATION

MACHINE PROCESS
SPI's ANALITICAL DATA STATISTICAL DATA SPO's PURE MATHEMATICS
RULES LAWS
— EMPIRICAL NUMBERS
— IMAGINARY
— STANDARDS &
— PROTOCOLS
— ANALOG & DIGITAL

HUMAN PROCESS
CRITICAL THINKING CONDITIONAL THINKING LOGICAL THINKING ANALITICAL THINKING
MULTITASKING COMPARATIVE THINKING

NOTES.

This is not the End.

www.ingramcontent.com/pod-product-compliance
Lightning Source LLC
LaVergne TN
LVHW022320060326
832902LV00020B/3585